MW01152620

SCOOBY-DOO!

An Estimation Mystery

THE CASE OF THE GREEDY GHOST

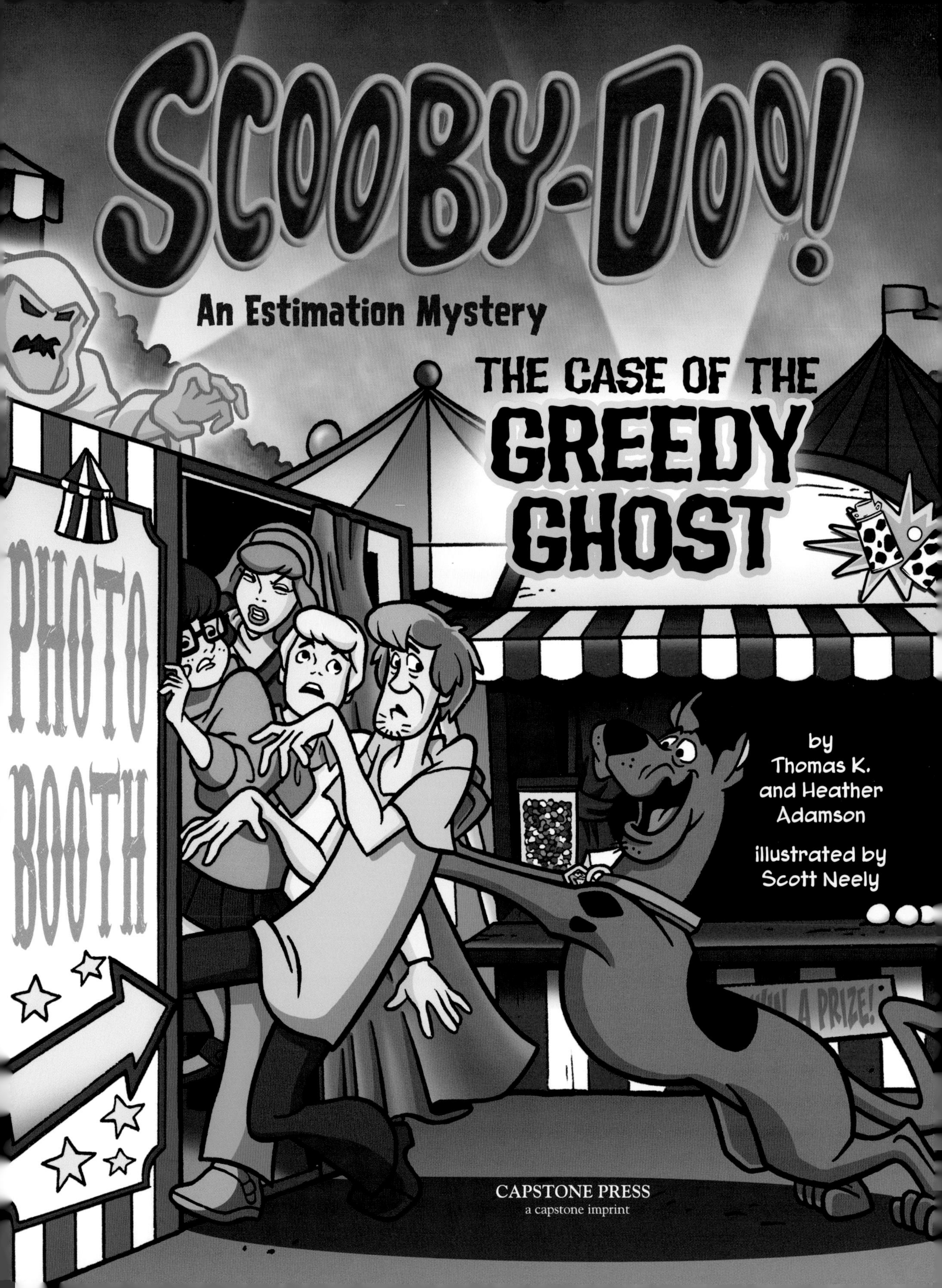

PHOTO BOOTH

by
Thomas K.
and Heather
Adamson

illustrated by
Scott Neely

WIN A PRIZE!

CAPSTONE PRESS
a capstone imprint

Published in 2018 by Capstone Press
A Capstone Imprint
1710 Roe Crest Drive
North Mankato, Minnesota 56003
www.mycapstone.com

Library of Congress Cataloging-in-Publication Data
Names: Adamson, Thomas K., 1970– author. | Adamson, Heather, 1974– author.
Title: Scooby-Doo! an estimation mystery : the case of the greedy ghost / by Thomas K.
and Heather Adamson.
Other titles: Case of the greedy ghost
Description: North Mankato, Minnesota : Capstone Press, a Capstone imprint, 2017. | Series:
Solve it with Scooby-Doo!: Math | Audience: Ages 5–7. | Audience: K to grade 3. | Includes
bibliographical references.
Identifiers: LCCN 2017002252 (print) | LCCN 2017009803 (ebook) | ISBN 9781515779056
(library hardcover) | ISBN 9781515779117 (eBook PDF)
Subjects: LCSH: Estimation theory—Juvenile literature. | Scooby-Doo (Fictitious character)—
Juvenile literature.
Classification: LCC QA276.8 .A335 2017 (print) | LCC QA276.8 (ebook) | DDC 519.5/44—dc23
LC record available at https://lccn.loc.gov/2017002252

Editor: Alesha Sullivan
Designer: Lori Bye
Art Director: Bob Lentz
Media Researcher: Svetlana Zhurkin
Production Specialist: Laura Manthe

The illustrations in this book were created digitally.

Printed in the United States of America.
010373F17

The Mystery Inc. gang helped their friend Rita set up for the Crystal Cove Fair. Their day began with a math problem as they worked on building a walkway to the Burger Shack. But Rita was secretly afraid to tell the gang the real reason she invited them to Crystal Cove. A ghostly creature was scaring all the visitors away.

Okay, gang, that's **5** boards in place.

Like, how many more to go until lunch break?

Velma scanned the distance to the Burger Shack. "I don't know exactly, but I bet we can estimate," she said.

Restirate?

Yes, Scooby-Doo. To estimate is to guess as close as possible. Estimating can save you time when an exact number isn't needed.

5 + 5 = 10

Daphne quickly estimated in her head. "If it took this much space for **5** boards, then . . . it looks like there's an equal distance to go. Do you know about how many total boards we will need?"

Rita needed to know how many people could stand on the new walkway. She didn't want the food line getting too crowded.

"Let's all stand on these 2 boards and see how much of the walkway we use," said Fred.

"That's 5 of us right here," replied Daphne. Velma looked at the amount of space the gang filled. Then, she looked at the amount of space left on the walkway.

Based on my calculations, I estimate 25 people could fit on the finished walkway.

Later on, the gang helped stock the Burger Shack with food. "Well, looks like there's enough ketchup!" said Daphne.

Shaggy drooled as he looked over all the boxes of food.

"Hey, Scoob, I bet that much ketchup could cover a lot of hot dogs!" said Shaggy.

"Reah! Rot Rogs — yum!" replied Scooby-Doo.

KETCHUP

KETCHUP

Approximately how many hot dogs do you think one bottle of ketchup would cover?

Scooby-Doo and the gang continued to prepare for the upcoming fair. All of a sudden, Rita broke down in tears. "I just hope we get any people at the fair at all," she wailed.

"Why do you say that, Rita?" asked Fred.

Rita paused. "Because a ghost is scaring all the visitors away."

Fred eyed the booth and took a guess.

Looks like only 3 people. Shaggy and Scooby, you go pretend to play the carnival games so the ghost will notice you.

Like, why are we always the bait?

13

Shaggy and Scooby-Doo walked through the rows of games. "Raggy, Rook! Ruckies," said Scooby.

"Like, that's a lot of ducks," said Shaggy. Shaggy read a sign that explained how the game worked. "It says: Pick a duck with a star to win a prize. Five winning ducks." Shaggy shrugged. "Like, how hard could it be to win?"

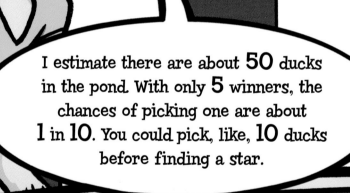

I estimate there are about 50 ducks in the pond. With only 5 winners, the chances of picking one are about 1 in 10. You could pick, like, 10 ducks before finding a star.

Suddenly, Scooby-Doo stopped in his tracks. "R-r-rrhost!!" he cried.

"Yeah, Scoob. We're waiting for the creepy ghost to scare us away," said Shaggy. Scooby's eyes widened, and he pointed. The ghost loomed behind Shaggy with a snarling glare.

Fred, Velma, and Daphne saw the ghost chasing Shaggy and Scooby toward them. "Get ready!" yelled Fred.

Rita ran to meet the Mystery Inc. gang near the photo booth. "You got him! Good work, gang!" she said.

"Let's find out who is trying to ruin the fair," said Fred.

Just then Rita pulled the sheet off the mysterious ghost. "Why, it's Chancy Roberts! Aren't you the local treasure hunter?"

So gang, who's up for some carnival games?

Looks like Shaggy and Scooby already found some prizes!

I think we're gonna need to get more prizes before the fair even starts.

Glossary

equal—being the same in number

estimate—to guess as close as possible

fair—a gathering in an open area with entertainment, amusements, and rides

meddling—busying oneself with something that is not one's concern

tablespoon—a large spoon used to serve food or as a measure in cooking

treasure—gold, jewels, money, or other valuable items that have been hidden

Internet Sites

Use FactHound to find Internet sites related to this book:

Visit www.facthound.com

Just type in this code 9781515779056 and go.

 **Super-cool stuff!** Check out projects, games and lots more at **www.capstonekids.com**